volume

7

Forests

OUR LIVING WORLD: EARTH'S BIOMES

Forests

Barbara A.
Somervill

TRADITION BOOKS®, MAPLE PLAIN, MINNESOTA

A NEW TRADITION IN CHILDREN'S PUBLISHING™

🖊 ABOUT THE AUTHOR

Barbara A. Somervill is the author

of many books for children. She loves

learning and sees every writing

project as a chance to learn new

information or gain a new under-

standing. Ms. Somervill grew up in

New York State, but has also lived in

Toronto, Canada; Canberra, Australia;

California; and South Carolina. She

currently lives with her husband in

Simpsonville, South Carolina.

🖊 CONTENT ADVISER

Susan Woodward, Professor of

Geography, Radford University,

Radford, Virginia

In gratitude to George R. Peterson Sr. for introducing me to the beauty of creation
—George R. Peterson Jr., Publisher, Tradition Books®

Published in the United States of America by Tradition Books® and distributed to the school and library market by The Child's World®

[ACKNOWLEDGMENTS]
For Editorial Directions, Inc.: E. Russell Primm, Editorial Director; Dana Meachen Rau, Line Editor; Katie Marsico, Associate Editor; Judi Shiffer, Associate Editor and Library Media Specialist; Matthew Messbarger, Editorial Assistant; Susan Hindman, Copy Editor; Lucia Raatma, Proofreaders; Ann Grau Duvall, Peter Garnham, Deborah Grahame, Katie Marsico, Elizabeth K. Martin, and Kathy Stevenson, Fact Checkers; Tim Griffin/IndexServ, Indexer; Cian Loughlin O'Day, Photo Researcher; Linda S. Koutris, Photo Selector

For The Design Lab: Kathleen Petelinsek, design, art direction, and cartography; Kari Thornborough, page production

[PHOTOS]
Cover/frontispiece: Darrell Gulin/Corbis.
Interior: Claudia Adams/Dembinsky Photo Associates: 30; Animals Animals/Earth Scenes: 31 (Studio Carlo Dani), 32 (Erwin & Peggy Bauer), 49 (Patti Murray), 52 (Michael Fogden), 57 (Scott W. Smith), 58 (Gerard Lacz), 60 (Peter Weimann), 61 (McDonald Wildlife Photography), 69 (Juergen and Christine Sohns), 70 (Manoj Shah), 72 (ABPL/Martin Harvey), 76 (John Anderson), 81 (OSF/Lon Lauber); Corbis: 8 (Robert Pickett), 22 (Kevin Schafer), 24 (Terry Whittaker; Frank Lane Picture Agency), 28 (Jim Zuckerman), 33 (Layne Kennedy), 41 (Peter Johnson), 48 (W. Perry Conway), 53 (Matt Brown), 66 (Tom Brakefield), 75 (Tim Zurowski), 78 (Patrick Bennett), 82 (Stuart Westmorland), 91 (Buddy Mays); Corbis Sygma: 84 (Ron Garrisson), 88 (Herve Collart); E. R. Degginger/Color-Pic: 62; Digital Vision: 10, 38, 40, 64, 85, 86; Michael & Patricia Fogden/Corbis: 11, 34, 44, 46; Gallo Images/Corbis: 15 (Roger De La Harpe), 43 (Anthony Bannister), 71 (Martin Harvey); Getty Images/Brand X Pictures: 55, 80; Martin Harvey/Corbis: 50, 74; Wolfgang Kaehler/Corbis: 36, 51, 77; Robert Maier/Animals Animals/Earth Scenes: 4, 42, 89; Photodisc: 6, 17, 18, 20, 21, 26, 35, 37, 73; Galen Rowell/Corbis: 9, 56; Keren Su/Corbis: 65, 83; Uwe Walz/Corbis: 29, 45.

[LIBRARY OF CONGRESS CATALOGING-IN-PUBLICATION DATA]
CIP data available

Table of Contents

Chapter One

Defining Forests

Beneath a silver fir tree, a pine marten catches a red squirrel. In the branches above, a crossbill pecks seeds from a cone. A black wood-pecker drills the bark in search of wood ants. Red deer browse on grasses in a nearby valley. A sparrow hawk shrieks as it glides above the treetops. Chatters, squeaks,

and trills fill Germany's Black Forest with sounds of life.

This is an old forest, with thick groves of spruce and silver fir. Willows drape over streams, and silver birches rise tall above green-gray juniper. In grassy meadows, pink rhododendrons turn toward the summer sun. Heather carpets a hillside with purple. This is a forest with a long history. One can only hope it will have an equally long future.

Types of Forests

🐿 Forest is land covered with closely spaced trees. The trees may be **coniferous, broadleaf evergreen,** or **deciduous.** While many coniferous trees are evergreen, not all ever-

▲ Germany's Black Forest

greens bear cones. Magnolias, holly, and boxwood are evergreens without cones. Cedars, spruce, cypress, and redwoods produce cones. Broadleaf trees include maples, birches, aspens, elms, oaks, beeches, and hickories. Deciduous broadleaf trees paint autumn forests with

> **? WORDS TO KNOW . . .**
>
> **broadleaf evergreen (BRAWD-leef EV-ur-green)** evergreen tree with broad leaves instead of needles
>
> **coniferous (kuh-NIF-ur-uhss)** bearing cones
>
> **deciduous (di-SIJ-oo-uhss)** annually dropping leaves or needles

◂ A pine marten slips beneath the trees in a German forest.

▲ Red, gold, and yellow color the leaves of a deciduous forest in the fall.

bright yellows, reds, and oranges.

Temperate Forests

🦎 Temperate climates feature hot summers and cold winters. **Precipitation** ranges from 10 to 30 inches (25 to 76 centimeters) yearly. Temperate forests appear

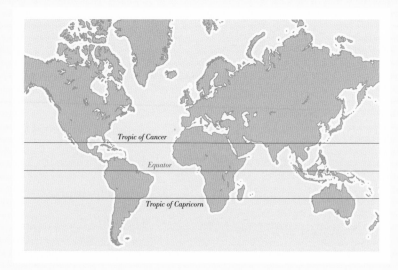

▲ The Tropic of Cancer, the equator, and the Tropic of Capricorn

in North America, South America, Europe, Asia, and Africa. On a map, these forests lie between the Arctic Circle and the Tropic of Cancer in the Northern Hemisphere. In the Southern Hemisphere, they lie between the Tropic of Capricorn and the Antarctic Circle.

▲ North America's temperate forests

▲ Wisent (European bison) live in forests, while American bison prefer the open grasslands.

oak, birch, maple, elm, or hickory are common. There are a multitude of these broadleaf deciduous trees in temperate forests. Elk, deer, moose, and wisent (European bison) live in temperate forests. Raccoons, squirrels, rabbits, weasels, foxes, and beavers also make homes there.

Taiga is a Russian word that refers to the marsh-filled forests of Siberia. Taiga—also called boreal ("northern") forest—is found in Russia but is located in northern Asia and North America, too. These forests have coniferous trees as well as broadleaf deciduous trees. They also contain moose, deer, wolves, and bears.

Temperate deciduous forests grow in eastern North America, western Europe, and eastern Asia. Areas of temperate deciduous forests usually have only two or three main kinds of trees. Large stands of

Temperate rain forests are fascinating. These forests

This Roosevelt elk cow and her calf graze in a meadow near Eureka, California. ▶

receive much more yearly rainfall than other temperate forests. Temperate rain forests stretch from west-central California to southern Alaska. They are also found in southern Chile. These forests receive more than 80 inches (203 cm) of precipitation each year. They have tall conifers found nowhere else on earth. Conifers are cone-bearing needleleaf trees. They contrast with broadleaf trees. Common trees in temperate rain forests include Douglas fir, sitka, spruce, western hemlock, and redwoods. Moss and lichen grow on tree trunks. Ferns are common on the forest floor. Eagles, spotted owls, cougars, and Roosevelt elk travel among the tall, ancient trees.

! WOULD YOU BELIEVE?

Redwoods can grow in "fairy rings." When a mature tree is cut down, new trees sprout from the stump. They form a circle of saplings—a fairy ring—from which new trees develop.

▲ Plant growth in a rain forest is so thick that little sunlight reaches the forest floor.

📖 **READ IT!**

Read all about the strange and fascinating world of rain forests in Toni Albert's book *The Remarkable Rain Forest: An Active-Learning Book for Kids* (Trickle Creek Books, 1996).

Tropical Forests

🐿 Tropical rain forests are found in Australia, Asia, South America, and Africa. Tropical rain forests lie close to the equator. Temperatures do not change much throughout the year. Rainfall averages 6.5 to 17 feet (2 to 5 meters) yearly. The climate is warm and wet. There are also deciduous sections of the tropics where there is a short dry season. The trees shed their leaves in the dry season. Both tropical rain forests and tropical dry forests have broadleaf trees. Tropical rain forests support incredible numbers of plants and animals. There are so many trees that two of the same species rarely grow next to each other. Most trees are broadleaf and evergreen. The tallest trees form a canopy that rises high above the forest floor. The topmost

layer of the tropical rain forest is the emergent layer. There are two lower canopies that make up the area below the **emergent** layer. Long vines, called lianas, drape from the upper canopy to the ground.

A rain forest supports hundreds of tree species and thousands of other plants as well as possibly millions of undiscovered species. Tropical rain forests support more than half the world's plant and animal species, while occupying only 6 to 7 percent of the earth's surface. Tropical rain forests have evergreen broadleaf trees, deciduous conifers, and needleleaf trees such as tamarack and bald cypress.

PROFILE: EPIPHYTES

Rain forests support many epiphytes. These unusual plants grow on trees and vines and can even grow on telephone wires in very wet climates. Their roots never touch the ground. They drink water and take in minerals from the air and rain. Epiphytes include many orchids, Spanish moss, and some ferns.

> **? WORDS TO KNOW . . .**
>
> **emergent (ih-MURR-juhnt)** appearing above the surface; in this case, above the canopy
>
> **epiphytes (EHP-uh-fites)** plants that get nutrition and water from the air and rain

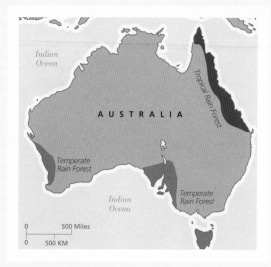

▲ Australia's rain forests and temperate forests

Forests around the World

🦎 In Australia, forests lie along the eastern coast. In the north, tropical rain forests grow much like the rain forests of Asia or Africa. Toward the south, forests contain scruffy pines (casuarina) and eucalyptus (gum trees). A trip from Canberra to the coast trails through a temperate pine forest, across dry scrub bush, then into a dense tree-fern forest.

Southern Asia and India have heavy rainfall and dense rain forests. Southeast Asia has mainly tropical rain forests, while India has tropical seasonal forests. Gibbons swing from tree to tree, hooting and howling. Orangutans live solitary lives, feasting on smelly durian

WOULD YOU BELIEVE?

The wettest place on earth is Assam, India. About 39 feet (11.9 m) of rain falls on this area every year.

More than a thousand different types of birds and hundreds of mammal species thrive in the wet world of the rain forest. Snakes and lizards climb through the trees. And insect species number in the tens of thousands. Many species in the rain forests have never been seen and, as yet, have no name.

fruit. Lizards, frogs, insects, and birds can be found everywhere, from the floor to the canopy. In northern Asia, boreal forests line the Pacific coast.

There, huge bears and Siberian tigers share the spruce and pine forests.

Europe has both temperate deciduous forests and taiga.

▲ Europe's temperate forests

Asia's boreal forests and rain forests

and fir forest. Across the Ural Mountains in Russia, dark green pines and spruce stand up to bitter, snowy winters.

African tropical rain forest is the stuff of Tarzan movies—although not all the animals that appear in those movies live in the jungle. A dense tangle of trees, vines, grasses, and shrubs covers much of western Africa. Because of the heavy **understory,** the jungle is considered a disturbed rain forest.

Taiga thrives in the cold weather of Norway, Sweden, Finland, and Russia. To the south, forests of birch, maple, and oak cover the Caucasus Mountains and western Europe. A surprising number of native azaleas add pinks and reds to the Caucasus in spring. In the Carpathian Mountains, lynxes, bears, wolves, and wildcats hunt through the mixed beech

Europe's boreal forests and temperate forests

14

(In contrast, an intact rain forest has a light understory.) The plant cover is so thick that humans must hack their way through with sharp knives called machetes. Heavy rainfall drums on leaves and branches, creating quite a racket. The African jungle supports dozens of species of monkeys and apes, hundreds of birds, and thousands of insects.

South and Central America also support dense tropical seasonal rain forests. They, too, have heavy, pounding rainfall for at least six months each year. Rain forest covers much of the northern half of the continent, between the Andes Mountains and the Atlantic Ocean. The Amazon River basin of South America

▲ This lush rain forest in South Africa supports thousands of insect, bird, and mammal species.

▲ Africa's rain forests

▲ South America's rain forests

is the location of the world's largest rain forest. Monkeys thrive in these forests. Brilliantly colored parrots and macaws feed on fruit and seeds throughout the rain forest. They share their home territories with slow-moving sloths and sleek jaguars.

North America has three types of forests: temperate rain forests, deciduous forests, and boreal forests. Rain forest lies along the western coast. It

includes Olympic National Park in Washington and Tongass National Forest in Alaska, the largest national forest in the United States. Deciduous forest runs along the Appalachian Mountains from northern Georgia to Maine. Most forests in Canada and central Alaska are boreal forests. Boreal forests have evergreen needleleaf trees. The dense spruce and fir support moose, weasels, and wolves.

▲ North America's boreal forests, rain forests, and temperate forests

Chapter Two

Focus on Key Species

☞ A gray wolf pack bounds through the deep snow of Yellowstone National Park. A moose senses the wolves' approach and bellows. The chase is on. Shots ring out. Two wolves fall dead upon the snow.

It is 1925. Predator control agents are rapidly killing off all wolves in the park. It is the job they were hired to do. In 1916, the National Park Service (NPS) began. One of its first acts was to rid

▲ A wolf pack sets out on a winter hunt.

Yellowstone of all predators, which are animals that kill and eat other animals. Wolves, coyotes, and cougars fell to the rifles of the control agents.

The newly formed NPS did not realize that nature provided a balance between predators and prey. Wolves, coyotes, and cougars rid the park of sickly, elderly, or injured moose and elk. Without those key predators, the moose and elk populations grew out of control. NPS changed its mind in 1933, but it was too late. By then, gray wolves were gone from Yellowstone's forest.

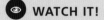 **WATCH IT!**

Watch the video *Yellowstone National Park* [ASIN: B00005TNFO] and learn about the elk, moose, wolves, gushing geysers, and bubbling mud pots of this park.

They had nearly disappeared from all the lower 48 states.

Keystone Species

A keystone species is an animal or plant that is crucial for the survival of an **ecosystem**. The species may change the land or create new habitats. The species may control prey populations. Or, it may be the main food of predators. In forests, some keystone species include wolves, quaking aspens, figs, and leaf-cutter ants.

Gray wolves are keystone predators. When 33 wolves were reintroduced to Yellowstone and 35 were released in Idaho in 1995 and 1996, they immediately changed

◄ Predators like this cougar help keep deer and elk herds healthy.

PROFILE: POLLINATORS

A pollinator is any creature that takes pollen from one flower and deposits it in another flower of the same type. Pollinators are keystone species in every land biome. Without pollinators, no flowers, honey, fruit, nuts, or vegetables would exist.

Between 130,000 and 200,000 pollinators live on the earth. Beetles pollinate nearly 90 percent of all flowering plants. Other pollinators include hummingbirds, bats, ants, wasps, bees, butterflies, and moths.

? WORDS TO KNOW . . .

biome (BYE-ohm) a large ecosystem in which the plants and animals are adapted to a particular climate or physical environment

ecosystem (EE-koh-siss-tuhm) a community of plants and animals and their relationship with the surrounding environment

▲ Quaking aspens provide a comfortable nursery for caterpillar and beetle larvae.

the wildlife population mix. Elk and moose herds actually benefited from being prey. Wolves killed off the weak, old, and sickly. The remaining healthy animals faced less competition for food.

Quaking aspens are important trees in many North American forests. The trees support a number of animal species. Caterpillars and beetle **larvae** depend on aspens as a safe "nursery" where they can grow. Deer, elk, rabbits, voles, mice, and wood rats eat aspen bark during the winter. Even hungry porcupines feed on aspen branches. Chickadees, warblers, nuthatches, and swallows nest in aspens.

In tropical rain forests, figs feed countless species. The regions of northeast Australia and many Pacific Islands feature strangler fig plants. Most tropical fruit trees produce fruit once or twice a year. But figs produce fruit all year long. This fruit feeds pigeons, parrots, toucans, monkeys, gibbons, bats, and hornbills. Butterflies and wasps feed on fig **nectar.** In some forests, nearly three-quarters of the local wildlife depend on fig trees for food.

Rain forest soil is extremely poor. Heavy rains wash away **nutrients.** Leaf-cutter ants recycle nature's

> **?** WORDS TO KNOW . . .
>
> **nectar (NEK-tur)** a sweet liquid found in flowers
>
> **nutrients (NOO-tree-uhnts)** substances needed by plants, animals, or humans for growth; key elements of a food

Porcupines climb trees to eat ▶ bark and branches.

nutrients. The ants snip leaves and carry them back to their nests. They use the leaves to feed fungus they grow for food. In the nests, dead leaves, fungus, and ant waste deposit nutrients into the soil. Leaf-cutter ants process about one-fifth of the leaves in their territory. Oddly, plants thrive because these ants trim their leaves.

Umbrella Species

Governments pass laws to protect **endangered** or **threatened** plants and animals. Legal protection stops people from hunting an animal or digging up or cutting down a plant. Umbrella species of the forests include bears, spotted owls, and rhinos—most especially the Javan and Sumatran rhinos.

An umbrella species is a protected animal or plant

◄ When leaf-cutter ants finish trimming this branch, the leaves will grow back.

that spreads its legal protection over other creatures. Usually these species feed over a large territory. Bears qualify as umbrella species. Several bear species are endangered in the wild. **Poaching,** overhunting, and loss of habitat have affected bear population growth.

Asiatic black bears live in Asia. They suffer from poachers who kill the animals for their paws and bile. Bear paws are used for medicine and to make soup. In Korea, Japan, and China, chefs prepare bear soup to serve in restaurants. Bear bile, from the animal's liver, is used to make medicinal products. The bile is taken out using painful and cruel methods during which the bear is confined. Asiatic black bears share their habitats with tigers, tarsiers, gibbons, and Asian water buffaloes. Laws set up to protect these bears also protect the other species in the region.

Spotted owls nest only in old-growth forests. They are endangered in the Pacific Northwest of the

READ IT!

They are fearsome beasts and gentle parents. Learn more about bears by reading Kennan Ward's *Grizzlies in the Wild* (NorthWood Press, 1994).

? WORDS TO KNOW . . .

poaching (POHCH-ing) hunting illegally

▲ The Asiatic black bear's territory

DO IT!

Help save the rhino! Find out what you can do at *http://www.rhinos-irf.org/how youncanhornin/index.htm.*

United States. Protection for spotted owls also protects trees that have lived for hundreds of years. Roosevelt elk and marbled murrelets, which are small sea birds, also prosper under the spotted owl's protective umbrella.

Javan and Sumatran rhinos are among the most endangered species of mammals. Most Javan rhinos live in the Ujong Kulon refuge on the island of Java. The refuge

supports 50 to 60 Javan rhinos. Another 8 to 10 Javan rhinos were found living in the wild in Vietnam. The Sumatran rhino total population stands at about 300 animals. Black rhinos are also endangered. The rhino horn is considered very valuable to poachers and is used for everything from knife handles to medicine. Legal protection is one way to save these species. When the rhinos have legal protection, all the other plants and creatures in their habitats survive.

Flagship Species

Flagship species are those that attract the public's attention. One of the most active programs for protecting a flag-

▲ The countries of Java and Sumatra

ship species is the "Save the Tiger" fund. This program, started by the National Fish and Wildlife Foundation in 1995, combines efforts from public businesses, zoos, national governments, law enforcement groups, and worldwide conservation groups. All tiger species are endangered, including the Siberian tiger that lives in the remote forests of northeast Asia.

◄ Zoos help preserve Sumatran rhinos. Loss of habitat has a negative affect on the species.

Tigers get plenty of attention. Nepal's Royal Chitwan National Park supports about 120 Bengal tigers. The Nepalese Army posts soldiers in the park to prevent poaching. The soldiers have been successful in protecting the tigers.

A flagship species of the rain forest is South America's golden lion tamarin. The National Zoo of the United States began a project to save the golden lion tamarin. They ran a captive-breeding program for tamarins. By the end of 2000, the zoo reintroduced 120 zoo-bred tamarins to the Poco das Antas Reserve in Brazil. Today, nearly 35 percent of Brazil's golden lion tamarins were either bred in the National Zoo or are related to zoo-bred tamarins.

The world's forests are filled with flagship species. In Australia, the koala is a popular forest animal. In Asia, Asian elephants, tigers, orangutans, and giant pandas are species that are the focus of major conservation programs. In North America, wolves and mountain lions receive plenty of attention.

The value of flagship species is that they generate interest and money. The interest helps pass laws to protect flagship species. The money sets up preserves and maintains breeding programs to keep endangered species alive.

> **WATCH IT!**
>
> Discover the beauty of the critically endangered Siberian tiger in National Geographic's *Tigers of the Snow* [ASIN: 6305572194].

◄ All tiger species are endangered in the wild, including the proud Siberian tiger.

Indicator Species

🦎 Indicator species measure the health of an ecosystem. Many species indicate, or show, biome problems. Pollution, overbuilding, erosion, or too much hunting and fishing change ecosystems. Indicator species measure those changes. Often, indicator species are insects, moths, and butterflies. However, larger species can also be indicator species.

The Javan gibbon lives in the rain forest canopy. Gibbons swing from tree to tree and rarely leave their high habitat. What happens when lumber companies cut down trees in the rain forest? The loss of trees breaks the

◀ The success of Javan gibbons tells scientists about the health of Indonesian rain forests.

closed canopy. Gibbons cannot travel from one area to another in search of food. When the gibbons die off, scientists know that the rain forest canopy is in danger.

Boreal owls serve as indicator species in the taiga of North America. The owls lay eggs in the spring. The number of eggs laid depends on the amount of food available. If boreal owls lay few eggs, that means their food supply is low. The owls eat mice, voles, and shrews. These rodents normally reproduce in large numbers. But rodent populations drop when drought limits food or when pollution poisons food in an area. Scientists know that if boreal owls leave their

▲ Boreal owls swoop through the trees of Russian taiga in search of mice and voles.

forest home, it is because that home is no longer a healthy environment.

Chapter Three

Predators

A beige-and-brown boa constrictor glides slowly along the rain forest floor in Venezuela. It is a full-sized adult, measuring nearly 20 feet (6.1 m) long. The boa has not eaten for a week and is looking for a meal. It coils itself among the fallen leaves and waits. The snake is too large to move quickly. It relies on patience to bring prey within its reach.

A careless white-lipped peccary walks by. The snake strikes. Boas do not rely on poison, but on power, to catch their prey. The snake wraps itself around the peccary and squeezes . . . and

▲ A male Siberian tiger may weigh up to 500 pounds (227 kilograms).

squeezes . . . and squeezes until the animal dies.

The boa will eat the peccary whole. Its jaws stretch wide enough to take in its prey. The peccary goes down head first, leaving a large lump in the snake's body. The effort involved in swallowing its prey exhausts the boa. It is time to rest. The boa will not need to feed again until next week, when another peccary might happen by.

Big Cats and Canines

🦎 Big cats and **canines** are the top predators of temperate and tropical forests. Cat species are active, stealthy hunters. Siberian tigers prowl the taiga of eastern Asia. Their distant

◀ An Amazon tree boa drops from a branch onto its prey. Boas squeeze their prey to death before eating them.

▲ This cougar silently stalks its prey.

relatives—mountain lions, bobcats, and lynxes—hunt in the boreal forests of North America. Mountain lions, leopards, and jaguars slip through the dense plant life of the rain forests.

Despite their reputation for hating water, big cats actually swim well. Siberian tigers always eat near water and often catch fish. Jaguars are excellent swimmers. They gladly follow prey into the water and usually outswim their victims.

Big cats eat meat. The prey they hunt depends on the size of the cat. Large cats hunt deer, elk, moose, wild pigs, and tapirs. Smaller cats, such as lynxes and bobcats, settle

for rabbits, hares, rodents, and ground-nesting birds. A large tiger would need to eat hundreds of mice to equal the meal provided by one deer.

Canines are basically dogs, such as foxes, coyotes, wolves, and bush dogs. Most canines hunt in groups, or packs. Wolves are the top predators among canines. A wolf pack may prefer elk and moose for dinner, but also consumes many rodents and hares.

Wolf packs are organized by rank. The pack leader is called the alpha male. His mate is the alpha female. Usually, they are the only pack members that have cubs. When wolf packs hunt, the alpha male eats first. Cubs quickly learn their table

RED WOLVES IN THE NEWS

Red wolves are native to the forests and mountains of the southeastern United States. Shortly after settlers arrived in colonial days, they began hunting red wolves. By 1960, only about 20 red wolves remained living in the wild.

The Red Wolf Recovery Program began to breed red wolves in zoos. The idea was to save the species and reintroduce it to the wild. Today, more than 100 red wolves roam the woods of eastern North Carolina, Mississippi, Florida, and South Carolina.

South America's poison arrow frogs have bright warning colors. These colors warn other animals not to take a bite. Each of these tiny creatures packs enough poison to kill 100 humans. Even licking the frogs can prove deadly. These frogs live on ants and spiders.

Poison arrow frogs have an unusual means of producing young. They lay about half a dozen eggs. The eggs hatch into tadpoles that quickly climb onto the mother's back. She deposits each tadpole in a pool of water held in leaves more than 100 feet (30 m) up in the canopy. She feeds her young by providing her own infertile eggs for them to eat. When the tadpole is a full-sized frog, it climbs out of the plant and hops away.

manners. If a cub tries to steal food from the pack leader, it gets a harsh growl and a swat.

Not Quite As Big

🐸 Predators do not have to be large to catch prey. Weasels, mongooses, martens, and wolverines are successful

▲ Wolverines store leftovers in underground pantries to eat later when food is scarce.

woodland predators. The mongoose is a daring hunter that specializes in killing snakes and scorpions. Martens, stoats, and weasels dine mainly on rodents. However, when rodents are scarce, they will eat earthworms, frogs, lizards, snakes, ground-nesting birds, and eggs.

Wolverines can kill prey larger than themselves. After they eat their fill, they bury their prey. When hunting is not successful, they dig up last month's deer from the underground pantry and eat what is left of it.

Smaller predators include animals that are insectivores—they eat insects. Insectivores include birds, rodents, and lizards. Chameleons are extremely efficient predators.

PROFILE: KOMODO DRAGON

The largest lizard—the Komodo dragon—lives on islands in and near Indonesia. These massive lizards grow up to 12 feet (3.7 m) long and weigh up to 300 pounds (136 kg). A Komodo dragon will stalk a water buffalo. It bites the buffalo's leg. The dragon's saliva is loaded with deadly bacteria. One bite kills even large animals. It may take the buffalo a week or two to die, but the dragon is patient. It will feast for several days off one buffalo.

They can blend their skin color with their surroundings. Chameleons have tongues that are as long as they are. A hungry chameleon perches in a conveniently hidden spot and waits for insects. An unsuspecting grasshopper leaps past, and the chameleon's tongue flicks out to catch dinner.

Insect eaters range from large anteaters and armadillos to tiny spiders. Many birds, such as woodpeckers, warblers, and flycatchers feed on insects. In Australia's forests, the superb lyrebird rummages under rotting logs to find tasty insects, beetles, and spiders.

Tiny shrews shuffle through the undergrowth on the forest floor. They are hunting for mites, beetles,

▲ An osprey's excellent vision allows it to see fish under the surface of lakes and ponds.

earwigs, and woodborers. Centipedes scuttle over dead leaves and branches in search of insects and spiders. They inject poison into their victims to paralyze them.

Birds That Hunt

Swift, accurate, and deadly, birds of prey are the premier hunters of the

! WOULD YOU BELIEVE?

Rain forests are full of blood-sucking critters. Among the common blood drinkers are vampire bats, mosquitoes, and several fly species.

Another bloodsucker is the leech. Leeches inject a painkiller when they bite their victims. More than 300 different types of leeches live in rain forests. The largest measures more than 8 inches (20 cm) long.

▲ African spotted eagle owls live on a diet of small rodents.

forests. Owls, goshawks, eagles, and osprey hover above the forest on nearly every continent. They feed on fish, rodents, snakes, and monkeys.

Owls generally hunt at night. They use excellent night vision to see mice, voles, shrews, and other creatures creeping about in the dark. The eagle owl is one of the largest owls. Eagle owls live in Europe, Asia, and northern Africa. They eat a variety of prey, including birds, reptiles, frogs, toads, fish, and spiders.

Great gray owls and boreal owls live in the taiga. They feed mostly on small voles. Owls eat their food whole, then spit up a pellet. The pellet contains bones, fur, and other indigestible parts of their meals.

PROFILE: A DANGEROUS PREDATOR

Once upon a time, flocks of passenger pigeons fluttered through the old growth forests of eastern North America. The pigeons numbered in the millions.

In 1813, naturalist John James Audubon described a flock of passenger pigeons in flight: "The light of the noonday sun was obscured as by an eclipse. . . . The pigeons were still passing . . . for three days in succession. . . . The banks of the Ohio were crowded with men and boys, incessantly shooting at the pilgrims [pigeons]."

Pigeons were hunted commercially for food and sport. At the same time, forests were cleared for farms. The flocks decreased rapidly because of all these factors. By 1896, only one major flock existed. Hunters killed 245,000 of the 250,000 birds in that flock. In 1900, the last passenger pigeon in the wild was shot. An entire species fell to their most dangerous predator—humans.

Goshawks fly the forest skies in North America, Europe, and Asia. Goshawks have amazingly quick reflexes. They can dart through dense forests and scoop up rabbits, squirrels, and pigeons.

The harpy eagle dominates the South American rain forest. This predator can weigh up to 15.5 pounds (7 kg). Harpies are fast, fearless, and agile. They dart between trees in search of monkeys, sloths, porcupines, and snakes.

In southern Asia, Bonelli's eagles glide through the air. Bonelli's eagles often kill prey that weighs as much or more than they do. They are powerful fliers that have no trouble bringing ducks, gulls, herons,

◀ Goshawks are common raptors in Europe, North America, and northern Asia.

and rabbits back to their nests. Africa's main forest eagle is the crowned eagle. Crowned eagles hunt in pairs and can bring down a young antelope or monkey.

▲ A Bonelli's eagle can fell prey that weighs more than it does.

Chapter Four

Prey

🐁 A wood mouse emerges from its burrow. Although they are the most common mice in Europe, wood mice are rarely seen. Even bright moonlight stops them from searching for food. Shyness helps the wood mouse survive. These mice are a major food source for foxes, weasels, and owls.

Female wood mice breed once they weigh about half an ounce (14 grams). They

produce four litters of young per year. One female delivers four to seven babies per litter, or about 16 to 28 young per year. The high rate of **reproduction** is necessary. Wood mice have a life span of about one year. To keep the species going, wood mice must produce enough young to survive predators, long winters, and short life spans.

Prey by the Numbers

Predators don't necessarily need to eat one large animal to feel full. It's a matter of how many prey make up a complete meal. A weasel may eat one squirrel, five wood mice, or hundreds of frog eggs. Thousands of insects breed millions of potential

PROFILE: TRAP-DOOR SPIDERS

Trap-door spiders are aggressive hunters. They build burrows that they cover with trapdoors made of spider silk, soil, and leaves. When unsuspecting prey pass by, the spiders pounce.

These same spiders become prey when a spider-hunting wasp comes around. The small wasp can turn the much larger spider into its victim. It stings the spider and paralyzes it. Then the wasp lays a single egg on the spider. The wasp larvae eat the spider alive.

> **? WORDS TO KNOW . . .**
>
> reproduction (ree-pruh-DUHK-shuhn) the act of having offspring

◄ This tiny wood mouse huddles beneath a woodland mushroom.

▲ Green anoles use their long toes to help them climb trees.

? WORDS TO KNOW . . .

carnivores (KAR-nuh-vorz)

animals that eat meat

◉ WATCH IT!

Uncover the links that tie rain

forest animals together. Watch

National Geographic's *Amazon:*

Land of the Flooded Forest

[ASIN: 6304473869].

meals for predators. Each insect species feeds birds, lizards, frogs, toads, snakes, rodents, and mammals.

Rodents are frequently on **carnivores'** dinner menus. Small rodents, such as mice, shrews, and chipmunks, feed foxes, weasels, and many birds of prey.

Reptiles and amphibians make excellent eating. Geckos, anoles, nonpoisonous snakes, frogs, and toads are tasty treats. They feed mammals, birds, and larger reptiles and amphibians.

Many animals appear to

have no natural enemies, yet they will become prey at some point in their lives. Sickness and age make top predators open to attack by smaller, younger predators. Mountain lions and wolves hunt individual coyotes. A pair of coyotes may turn the tables and hunt injured mountain lions or wolves.

Death turns every animal into food for others. **Carrion** feeders, such as buzzards and vultures, eat dead animals. Insects join the feast and may lay their

▲ This bird may look like a hawk, but it is actually a Eurasian buzzard.

▲ The enemies of this eyed silk moth of Costa Rica see the eyes of a predator—not the wings of a defenseless moth.

eggs in the flesh. Even bones provide nutrition. A porcupine will gnaw bones or dropped antlers for calcium and protein.

Building Up Defenses

🦎 Coloring and camouflage hide prey from their enemies. The leaf or horned frog looks exactly like dead leaves on a forest floor. Goldenrod spiders appear to be tiny yellow flowers. Stick insects can barely be seen among tall grass or twigs of the rain forest.

Some animals look or act like another species. Viceroy butterflies look much like monarch butterflies. Because monarchs taste terrible, few predators try eating viceroys, either. A Costa Rican eyed silk moth looks more like the face of a larger animal. The moth's wings feature designs that look like eyes. The "face" frightens potential predators.

Poison and bright colors make excellent partners for protection. Fire salamanders and poison arrow frogs have bright colors. The coloring warns other animals: Don't eat me, I'm deadly.

When all else fails, smart creatures run away. The Malayan flying frog heaves itself from a branch high in the rain forest canopy. The frog spreads its toes apart. Skin between the toes makes a parachute of sorts. The frog glides to another tree. Malayan

PROFILE: ARMY ANTS

Ants, as individuals, feed dozens of creatures. Anteaters, echidnas, and chimpanzees attack anthills and settle down for a feast. However, one ant species is more predator than prey.

Army ants of Peru and Brazil typically swarm over spiders, scorpions, beetles, and roaches for food. Once they have eaten every critter in their territory, they move camp. Any animal in their path becomes prey to the hungry ants. This can include lizards, snakes, chickens, pigs, and goats. Army ants swarm in the millions and have been know to devour 100,000 animals in one day's march.

▲ When this coyote dies, his carcass will become part of the food chain that keeps nature in balance.

Insects are the most abundant **herbivores.** Larger insects prey on smaller insects. Birds and lizards prey on insects regardless of size. Weasels and snakes prey on birds and lizards. Coyotes, bobcats, and leopards prey on weasels, snakes, birds, and lizards. In some regions, coyotes and bobcats may be the top predators. However, where mountain lions and wolves live, coyotes and bobcats become prey.

The food cycle depends on prey and predators. Without predators, prey would reproduce in massive numbers. Prey populations would soon take over lakes and streams. Predators keep prey population levels in check. This is another example of nature's balance.

? WORDS TO KNOW . . .

herbivores (HUR-buh-vorz)

animals that eat plants

---

flying frogs can cover about 100 feet (30 m) in one glide.

The Food Cycle

Here is an example of how the food web works. Plants form the base of the food web.

Chapter Five

Flora

Deep in the rain forests of Malaysia, rafflesia plants blossom. The rafflesia is a parasitic plant of the liana, a vine that roots in the ground. Because it is parasitic, the rafflesia invades the vine and feeds through its roots and stem. The rafflesia bud takes 10 months to burst into flower. When it does, the scent stinks like rotting meat. The stench has earned the rafflesia the nickname corpse flower.

▲ The rafflesia emits a stench of rotting meat to attract pollinators such as flies and bees.

▲ Every day, about 214,000 acres (86,000 hectares) of rain forest are cut down. This is an area larger than New York City.

The *Rafflesia arnoldii* is the world's largest flower. Its bright red blossom measures up to 36 inches (90 cm) across. It is a rare, endangered flower. Its rarity increases as Malaysian rain forests are cut down.

Another threat to the rafflesia is the sale of its buds in local markets. Malaysian folk medicine claims that the buds can help a mother recover after the birth of a child. Sellers have harvested so many of the buds that few rafflesias survive in the wild.

The Rain Forest by Layers

Rain forests grow in definite layers. At the bottom lies the forest floor. Along the tree

The rain forest canopy supports a complete ecosystem 100 feet (30 m) above the ▶ forest floor.

trunks grows the understory. A high canopy of branches and leaves rises above the understory. Still higher grow the emergent trees. More than 50,000 species of tropical trees live in rain forests around the world. Add to that more than 200,000 species of other flowering plants and thousands of ferns and mosses.

The forest floor supports countless species of flowers, herbs, shrubs, and vines. Plants at ground level must grow well in shade. Delicate ginger, passionflower, and strangely named hot-lips

flowers bloom among the rotting leaves of the rain forest floor. Lacy ferns and moss grow along the ground in temperate rain forests.

The understory features shrubs and short trees, such as palms, tree ferns, and southern beeches. Vines wrap around tree trunks. Hibiscus flowers brighten the understory with their bright rose-colored petals. Orchids of every color bloom throughout the year.

Densely packed leaves and branches form a thick canopy

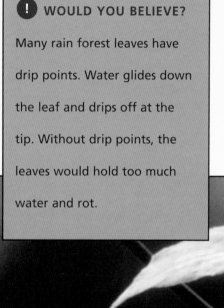

! WOULD YOU BELIEVE?

Many rain forest leaves have drip points. Water glides down the leaf and drips off at the tip. Without drip points, the leaves would hold too much water and rot.

that hoards rain and sunlight. Trees in the canopy reach from 60 to 130 feet (18 to 40 m) tall. Most have no branches in the understory. Temperate rain forests feature extremely tall evergreens, such as redwoods and Douglas fir.

Tropical rain forests have different tree species from temperate rain forests—and more of them. South American tropical rain forests may have as many as 120 trees per acre. One odd tropical tree is the strangler fig. It begins as an epiphyte, sending its roots down along the trunk of its host to the ground. As the fig grows, it kills the host tree by hogging its sunlight and nutrients.

▲ This Douglas fir is one of many extremely tall evergreens that grow in temperate rain forests.

Emergent trees grow beyond the top of the canopy. They may reach heights of 240 feet (73 m). The

! WOULD YOU BELIEVE?

The world's tallest redwood rises 365 feet (111 m) above the ground.

◀ Bright scarlet passionflowers attract butterflies and hummingbirds.

branches and leaves form an umbrella above the dense rain forest canopy.

Deciduous Forests

🐿 Temperate deciduous forests have far fewer plant species than tropical forests. Common trees include elm, maple, oak, aspen, and poplar. Temperate forests face four distinct seasons. Spring brings tender new leaves and blossoms to barren branches. In summer, the broad leaves fill out in various shapes and sizes. Summer is when most deciduous trees grow. In autumn, the leaves change color, die, and fall to the ground. Winter trees are like bears—they hibernate, or sleep, through the winter.

The floor of a deciduous forest is thick with rotting plant matter. Layers of dead leaves and fallen branches feed nutrients into the soil. Deep purple violets peep out from dark green leaves. Jack-in-the-pulpits pop up from the floor. Honeysuckle vines, blackberry bushes, and wild blueberries attract bees, birds, and bears. Ferns, mosses, and lichens cover open ground, rocks, and tree trunks.

Deciduous trees form a broken canopy above the forest floor. Trees die or are knocked down by strong winds. They burn in forest fires. The canopy allows sunlight to reach

🐇 LOOK IT UP!

Hike along a forest trail that stretches from Springer Mountain, Georgia, to Mount Katahdin, Maine. Discover the Appalachian Trail at *http://www. fred.net/kathy/at.html*.

▲ An ice storm turns barren tree branches into a lacy winter wonderland.

the forest floor. Breaks in the forest allow grass meadows to develop. The meadows last only as long as it takes young trees to reach maturity.

Taiga

The taiga, or boreal forest, also has four seasons. Winter is the longest season and presents

▲ Moss covers the floor of this boreal forest.

many demands. Evergreen trees collect snow on their branches. The snow can become so heavy that the branches crack from the weight. The forest floor may be buried several feet deep in snow. Spring brings the thaw. Snow melts and leaves the ground spongy and wet. Summer provides a short growing season, usually no more than six to ten weeks. Autumn comes early, and the taiga prepares again for the long winter ahead.

The taiga forest floor has few flowering plants. Lady slipper orchids, berry bushes, and calypso orchids are scattered

📖 READ IT!

Learn more about boreal forests. Read Elizabeth Kaplan's *Taiga* (Benchmark, 1996).

throughout taiga forests. Most taiga forest floors feature mosses, fungus, and lichens.

Most taiga trees are coniferous. There are 530 species of conifers. (Not all grow in the taiga.) This is far fewer than the 50,000 species of tropical broadleaf trees. Conifers include spruces, firs, pines, cedars, tamarack, and junipers.

Taiga trees tend to be shorter than trees in rain forests or deciduous forests. Bitter winters, strong winds, and lower precipitation determine the types and sizes of trees in boreal forests. Deciduous aspen, birch, and balsam poplar grow in taiga forests. In autumn, these trees paint bands of gold against the dark green of taiga conifers.

PROFILE: CARNIVOROUS PLANTS

Meat-eating plants catch insects and spiders for dinner. These plants are found in bogs in the taiga. The pitcher plant is like a narrow jar with liquid at the bottom. Insects lured onto the pitcher's edge fall in and drown. Bog violets and sundews (above) have sticky goo on their leaves and stems. Insects that touch the glue are stuck. The leaves wrap around the prey, and the plant digests it.

Chapter Six

Herbivores

🦎 A tiny newborn koala pulls itself toward its mother's pouch. The baby is about the size of a nickel. Once in the pouch, it will drink its mother's milk.

Mom is not disturbed by the birth. She is nestled in the branches of a eucalyptus

▲ Koalas never drink water. Instead, they get liquid from the eucalyptus leaves they eat each day.

tree in Queensland, Australia. It is night, which means it is feeding time. She slowly munches tender leaves and sprouting twigs.

Most people do not know much about koalas. They are **marsupials,** not bears. They eat eucalyptus, but not all types. Of the 500 varieties of eucalyptus, koalas feed on only 12 of them. The name *koala* comes from the Australian Aboriginal language. It means "no drink." It is a good name for an animal that never drinks.

Plant Eaters

Herbivores are among the largest animals of the forest. In Asian rain forests, the Asian elephant, Javan rhino, and Sumatran rhino feed on grasses and reeds. Giant pandas of China eat only bamboo.

In boreal forests, moose, elk, and deer graze in open meadows. They retreat deep into the woods during winter and gnaw tree bark. Beavers chew through tree trunks. Always efficient, beavers use the trunks for building their lodges, and eat the leaves and tender shoots as food.

Bears, although usually listed as carnivores, are actually **omnivores.** The diet of many bears is about 80 percent plants and only 20 percent

? WORDS TO KNOW . . .

marsupials (mahr-SOO-pee-uhlz) order of animals in which the young develop in pouches on the mother's body

omnivores (OM-nuh-vorz) animals that eat both plants and meat

📖 READ IT!

Follow deer into the deep woods in Carl R. Sams's *Stranger in the Woods* (self-published, 2000).

meat. A grizzly in a feeding frenzy may gorge itself on 200,000 berries in one day. Scientists studied brown and black bears in Glacier National Park in West Glacier, Montana. They found that the bears ate mostly grass, cow parsnips, flowering plants, and huckleberries.

Pygmy marmosets, the smallest South American primates, suck sap from tree trunks and eat fruit and insects. Tamarins also eat fruit and insects, as well as small lizards, frogs, and snails. Black-bearded sakis eat fruit, nuts, and seeds in the upper canopy. Squirrel monkeys feed on fruit and flowers.

◄ Pygmy marmosets weigh about 3 ounces (85 g). One could fit in the palm of your hand.

Fruit, Nuts, Seeds, and Nectar

Animals that eat fruit, nuts, seeds, or nectar live in every forest biome. Several bat species feed only on fruit. The Indian flying fox loves mangoes, guavas, and bananas. Bats enjoy soft, overripe fruit. They suck the juice and eat the pulp, spitting out the tough outer skin.

In boreal forests, pine-cones and needles from spruce and fir trees litter the floor. One cone contains many seeds—a feast for mice and voles. In some years in temperate deciduous forests, oaks produce bumper crops of acorns. Squirrels exhaust themselves collecting thou-

▲ The Indian flying fox—actually a bat—has a wingspan of more than 4 feet (1.2 m).

sands of acorns to last the long winter months.

Forest flowers attract bees, butterflies, and hummingbirds. They drink the nectar held in flowers. Hummingbirds are attracted by the color red.

PROFILE: MORPHOS BUTTERFLY

The Morphos butterfly (above) searches the Amazon rain forest for rotting fruit—its favorite meal. These large butterflies have a wingspan of up to 7 inches (17.8 cm) across. The females are a dull brown, but males are a stunningly beautiful blue.

They will pass by yellow or white flowers to zero in on red blossoms.

Many birds feed on seeds and fruit. Seed-eating birds of boreal and deciduous forests include swallows and pigeons. Compared to their rain forest relatives, these birds are dull in color.

Parrots, toucans, cocka- toos, macaws, and rosellas

spread their wings in tropical rain forests. Their startling reds, yellows, blues, and greens delight the eye. South American macaw feathers range from bright green to vivid blue and yellow. Macaws can break open the toughest nuts with their powerful beaks. They also eat fruit and berries.

Eclectus parrots come in two distinct shades. Females are blue and bright red. Males are brilliant green. Eclectus parrots live in northern Australia, New Guinea, and the Solomon Islands. They feed on treetop seeds, nuts, and flowers.

Decomposers

🐇 Every forest floor collects dead leaves and branches, rotting fruit, fallen animal parts,

▲ Cape York, Australia; New Guinea; and the Solomon Islands

and feces. A group of animals and plants feed on the trash littering the forest floor. They are called decomposers. Decomposers recycle forest trash into fertilized, healthy soil.

Consider a typical forest floor. Worms feast on dead leaves. They produce large amounts of solid waste that

📖 **READ IT!**

Learn more about parrots in Mark J. Rauzon's *Parrots around the World* (Franklin Watts, 2001).

▲ Millipedes are decomposers. They feed on rotting plants and leaves on the forest floor.

deposit nutrients into the soil. Not all worms are small. The largest earthworm measures up to 11 feet (3.4 m) long. Slugs and snails leave trails of slime behind them as they search for tasty plants. This slime contains nutrients that are good for plants. They will eat living plants and freshly fallen leaves.

Nearby, termites munch their way through a fallen tree limb. A millipede crawls over the forest litter. It settles on rotting fruit for a meal. Dung beetles collect feces from other animals. They roll the waste into balls and lay their eggs inside. Their larvae feed on the dung.

Chapter Seven

A Cycle of Life

🐾 A mother orangutan clings to a scrawny female infant. She will be a single parent, raising this youngster for nearly eight

▲ A baby orangutan practices swinging from a branch.

years. The mother already has one child, a six-year-old **juvenile** male. He is playful and pokes at the newborn. His mother gives him a gentle swat.

Orangutans have a long childhood. The baby will nurse until she is about three.

Mother is family, teacher, feeder, and groomer for her young.

An adult female has two or three young during her lifetime. This slow rate of reproduction, along with the loss of habitat and food source, has put the species in danger of **extinction.** Female orangutans have been killed so that their young can be placed in zoos.

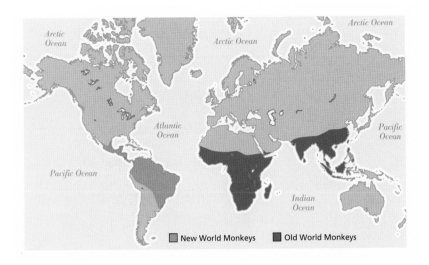

▲ The territory of old world monkeys and new world monkeys

The loss of every orangutan is crucial.

The Great Apes

Great apes belong to the **primate** family, just like humans. Primates are divided into two groups: **prosimians** and **simians.** Prosimians have snouts that stick out, much like a dog's. These include lemurs and lorises, which live in Africa and Asia. Simians include monkeys and apes. Simians live in Asia, Africa, and South America.

Monkeys and apes fall into either "new world" or "old world" groups. New world primates live in rain forests of Central and South America. Tiny pygmy marmosets and elegant golden lion tamarins are

◄ Mother and child orangutans share a special bond—just like human mothers and their babies.

new world primates. Old world primates live in Africa and Asia. They include the great apes: chimpanzees, gorillas, and orangutans.

Chimpanzees are the smallest great apes. An average male weighs 100 to 175 pounds (45 to 79 kg) and stands 5.5 feet (1.7 m) tall. Chimpanzees live in African forests in social groups called troops. A troop has 25 to 75 individuals. Chimpanzees eat mainly fruit but will snack on ants, termites, and honey. Chimps also hunt and kill other primates, including colobus monkeys and baboons.

Gorillas are the largest apes. They, too, live in Africa. A full-sized adult male can weigh up to 400 pounds (180 kg). Males are called silverbacks because the hair on their backs turns gray in adulthood. Gorillas are peaceful creatures. They will groom one another (pick insects from fur) for hours. This activity is so relaxing that it often puts the groomed ape to sleep. Gorillas live in family groups with one or more males and up to 30 females and their young.

Orangutans, also called orangs, live only on the islands of Borneo and Sumatra. The word *orangutan* means "man of the forest." Indeed, orangs are the closest apes to humans. More than 95 percent of the genes that make up orangs are also found in humans. Orangs eat fruit and travel a large territory to find their food.

This silverback gorilla is probably the dominant male in his family. ▶

From Birth to Adulthood

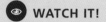 A newborn great ape begins life clinging to its mother's belly. It will nurse at its mother's breast for many months. Orangs nurse longest and are weaned at about three years old.

Apes are excellent parents. They take good care of their children. This is important because the children depend on their parents for food, shelter, and protection. A chimpanzee juvenile will be

● WATCH IT!

Swing with the best—watch Dorling Kindersley's *Amazing Animals: Monkeys and Apes* [ASIN: 0789421542].

totally dependent on its mother for at least two years.

Playing is an important part of ape childhood. Play gives young apes practice climbing, swinging, and hanging from limbs. Young orangutans must strengthen their arms and legs for a lifetime in the canopy. Young orangs are particularly open to attack on the ground. They rarely leave their leafy homes in the trees.

Lessons Learned

⌘ Ape mothers teach youngsters where to find food. Juveniles must learn what can be eaten safely and what is poisonous. Mothers develop close relationships with other troop members. Aunts, sisters, and grandmothers may take turns

PROFILE: TOOLS AND CHIMPS

Chimpanzees use tools to help them in their daily lives. They use sticks like fishing poles to catch ants and termites. The insects hold on to the stick and end up as a snack. Large sticks become clubs to fend off enemies or attackers. Chimps catch water for drinking by making leaf cups. They also use leaves to make nests for sleeping each night. Rocks make excellent nutcrackers and fruit openers.

◄ Chimpanzees are clever, agile, and fun-loving.

▲ Chimpanzees form a social bond by grooming each other.

caring for young gorillas and chimpanzees. Orangs, on the other hand, have few social relationships.

Young apes must learn to recognize danger. Chimpanzees have several natural enemies. Leopards attack chimp juveniles. The chimps shout warnings and make frightening faces when danger comes.

In ape troops, social rank and manners are important. One way apes show closeness is by grooming one another. As apes grow, they learn their place in the troop. The youngsters must accept the rules of the male troop leader.

Adults in the Ape World

🐒 Once they reach adulthood, males and females travel separate routes. Males leave

The orangutan is Asia's only great ape. ▶

the troop and find their own territories. A lucky male will find a female willing to start a family away from her troop. Once a male becomes elderly, other troop members treat him with respect.

Females have very free lives. They may stay with the troop they grew up with or move to join other troops. Sometimes a female will accept a lone male, and together they become the founding parents of a new troop. The female has already learned

LOOK IT UP!

What is being done to save the great apes from extinction? Visit the Ape Alliance and find out at *http://www.4apes.com/gorilla*.

▲ Rangers look for gorilla traps and dismantle them. Poaching continues to endanger gorillas.

the great apes is humans. Gorillas are killed for their hands and heads (which are then sold as souvenirs and ornaments), their meat, and for sport. Orangs are forced from their homes by logging companies. Chimpanzees are captured for use in medical labs and for sale as pets.

Worldwide bans on the sale of these animals have had little effect. Poaching pays good money. Many people in Central Africa depend on ape meat for food. Hungry people do not see the value in saving apes while they starve. But conservation groups are winning the battle. Hopefully, they will win the war before the great apes are gone forever.

parenting skills by watching the other females in her birth troop.

Gorillas may live 35 years in the wild. Orangs also live about 35 years. Chimpanzees have a life span of 40 to 50 years. The greatest threat to

The Old-Growth Forest

Sunlight trickles through giant redwood branches. A plump Douglas squirrel skitters up the side of a tree that towers nearly 250 feet (76.2 m) high. A blue Steller's jay darts through the old-growth forest. The jay snatches an egg from the nest of a marbled murrelet.

The forest floor lies spongy with moss and fallen leaves. A bright

▲ Steller's jays depend on old-growth forest for survival.

> **! WOULD YOU BELIEVE?**
>
> A mature redwood produces thousands of seed cones each year. Only one seed in a million becomes a mature redwood tree.

yellow banana slug oozes its way over the dead leaves, leaving a trail of slime.

The slug disappears beneath wisps of maidenhair fern. Wind shifts the branches above. A shower of tiny cones drops to the ground with soft thuds.

Inside the redwood's trunk, rings record its 1,000-year history. Forest fires have left burned scars. Narrow rings tell of periods with little water. Thick rings report years with heavy rainfall. Dark speckles are lasting reminders of insects that crawled on this tree centuries ago.

Defining the Old-Growth Forest

An old-growth forest has plants that have grown without human interference. That interference could be from building roads or, most often,

◄ Some redwood trees in Jedediah Smith State Park, California, may be more than 1,000 years old.

▲ The Ecuadorian rain forest provides a safe haven for this young crested owl.

from logging or clearing land for farming or housing. Old-growth trees are more than 250 years old. The forest contains trees at various stages of growth. Broken tree stumps, called snags, stand beneath breaks in the canopy. Fallen trees lie slowly rotting on the forest floor.

Ancient forests exist on every continent where forests grow. The Amazon rain forest, forests in western Australia, the Congo rain forest, and the Siberian taiga are old-growth

(!) WOULD YOU BELIEVE?

Scientists studied 20 marri trees in an Australian old-growth forest. They discovered that each tree supported an average of 443 insect species. Many of these species were new to the scientists and hadn't even been named.

TIME LINE:

A redwood seed takes hold.	A.D. 03
Great Plains Native Americans develop the bow and arrow.	500–650
Viking Leif Eriksson lands on North American soil.	1000
Christopher Columbus sails to the "New World."	1492
The Jamestown colony is settled.	1607
The Declaration of Independence is signed.	1776
The California gold rush occurs.	1849
A 2,000-year-old tree is cut by loggers.	2003

forests. In North America, old-growth forests are a living history of our continent.

Trees sprout, grow, and die. In between, they feed rodents, birds, deer, and elk. They shelter sparrows, jays, and endangered marbled murrelets. When they die, they topple to the ground. Dead trees may take 500 years to decay. During that time, countless

◀ Giant redwoods tower over forest activity.

insects, snails, birds, and mammals feed on, nest in, and shelter beneath the trunks.

Why Save Ancient Forests?

✍ Some people believe that a tree is a tree is a tree. They think that cutting down old trees doesn't matter. People can always plant new trees. This is wrong. It takes nearly 1,000 years for the natural balance of an old-growth forest to develop. Loss of that balance cannot be replaced in 5 years . . . 50 years . . . or even 500 years.

Humans need forest products. They heat their homes, eat food, drink water, build furniture, and take medicine. Forests help them do these

TONGASS FOREST IN THE NEWS

The Tongass National Forest in Alaska is the largest national forest in the United States. It covers 17 million acres (6.9 million hectares) and supports deer, moose, bears, wolves, salmon, and bald eagles.

Under current plans, only 676,000 acres (274,000 hectares)—less than 10 percent of the total forest—may be harvested over the next 100 years. Loss of old-growth forest is much like a tumbling house of cards. Scientists estimate that logging will reduce deer populations by three-quarters. This means local wolves will lose a major food source. Bald eagles will lose almost all of their nesting and perching places. They feed on salmon in local rivers. Salmon depend on the forest to keep river water clean where they lay their eggs. Without clean water, the salmon population will decline. Bears that eat salmon to fatten themselves for their long winter sleep will suffer.

READ IT!

Learn more about the bird that may save the old-growth forest. Read *Spotted Owl: Bird of the Ancient Forest* by Brenda Z. Guiberson (Henry Holt, 1994).

things. Like wetlands, forests clean and renew water sources. They provide fruit, nuts, and berries. Animals that roam the forests may provide food for people.

Many medicines humans take today come from old-growth forest plants.

Clear-cutting all the trees, burning the undergrowth, and

logging may destroy animal and plant species that are yet unknown. It is possible that the cure for a deadly disease is growing today in an old-growth forest. That plant may be destroyed before people even know it exists.

Ninety percent of North American trees to be cut this year stand in old-growth forests. Conservationists want to stop cutting in old-growth forests. They chose one endangered species as a symbol of ancient forests in North America: the northern spotted owl. Spotted owls cannot survive without the old-growth ecosystem.

Laws now protect up to 550 pairs of owls in northern California. About 1,000

▲ Laws protect this northern spotted owl and its habitat.

acres (405 hectares) of ancient forest are set aside for each breeding pair. Spotted owls are umbrella species of North American old-growth forests. Roosevelt elks, wolves, marbled murrelets, and other

◄ About 10,000 bald eagles nest in the treetops of Tongass National Forest.

▲ Clear-cutting in the Tongass National Forest leaves the land vulnerable to erosion.

endangered species fall under the spotted owl's umbrella of safety.

In the United States, logging cuts about 175 acres (71 hectares) of ancient forest each day. Nearly 10 percent of South America's rain forest has fallen under the axe. In Malaysia, the minister of the environment holds the most licenses for cutting timber in valued rain forest regions. Logging continues there at a record pace. Canadian timber companies hold leases for cutting trees in more than 90 percent of Canada's government-run ancient forests. Logging in old-growth forests continues at alarming rates. Legal action takes time and cannot always catch up to the logger's chain saws.

Chapter Nine

The Human Touch

🐾 A giant panda lumbers through the bamboo forest of Sichuan province, China. This 220-pound (100-kg) animal eats leaves, shoots, and branches of bamboo for 18 hours a day. As a food, bamboo has little nutrition. Each day, the panda must eat at least 30 pounds (13.6 kg) of bamboo. But they can eat as much as 85 pounds (39 kg) of bamboo shoots daily. They can also weigh as much as 300 pounds (136 kg).

▲ Giant panda habitats slowly disappear as China's population takes over the bamboo forests.

▲ The survival of the giant panda depends on successful births in captivity. Week-old Hua Mei was born in the San Diego Zoo.

LOOK IT UP!

Watch the antics of young Hua Mei or learn about the other pandas at the San Diego Zoo. Visit the zoo Web site, *http://www.sandiegozoo. org/pandas*.

At one point, the world population of giant pandas dropped below 300. With a current world population of about 1,000, the species is still considered extremely endangered. Loss of forest habitat is the panda's greatest danger.

In a joint effort among Chinese scientists, the San Diego Zoo, and the National Zoo in Washington, D.C., people have been trying to breed pandas in zoos. In San Diego, Hua Mei became the fifth giant panda born in captivity in the United States. Her survival may signal hope for saving this rare and amazing species.

Much rain forest timber from Malaysia is turned into disposable chopsticks when it ▶ reaches Japan.

Threats to the World's Forests

 Threats to the world's forests are many. Logging, clear-cutting, and planned burning destroy many acres of forests each day. Pollution kills plants and animals. The sale of rare, endangered, and threatened animals continues on a large scale.

Conservation groups try to control these threats. However, it is impossible to prevent everything that damages the environment. Setting up preserves, national forests, and protected wilderness areas helps but does not cure

▲ Logging in the Philippines provides jobs and clears land for crops, but at what cost?

environmental ills. Laws protecting endangered and threatened species reduce poaching but do not prevent poaching completely.

Cutting the Forests

Rain forests grow in many countries that have few other resources. Governments of those countries often do not think twice about cutting trees. Trees equal money. Logs are sold for building and furniture making and as pulp for paper. Much of Malaysia's lumber is sold to Japan to make disposable chopsticks.

Rain forest is often clear-cut to create cattle pastures. Loss of habitat affects the plants and animals of the region. However, rain forest grazing produces beef that is less expensive than beef from other countries. Cheap beef provides the burgers served by fast-food restaurants in North America.

Loss of plant growth increases soil erosion. Topsoil needed for growing plants gets washed into local streams and rivers. Soil erosion clouds rivers, creating added problems for fish and river plants. Cloudy water prevents sunshine from reaching the river bottom. Plants and animals living on the riverbed struggle to survive.

Pollution and the Forests

Plant matter is burned to clear land. Smoke puts carbon monoxide and carbon dioxide into the air. The smoke results in polluted air and acid rain, another form of chemical pollution. Acid rain also comes from burning fossil fuels, such as oil, gasoline, or coal. Humans use fossil fuels to power cars and trucks, heat homes, and run factories. Burned fuel produces **emissions** that contain sulfur, nitrogen, and chlorine. These are basic chemical elements found in nature.

The acid is formed when certain amounts of sulfur,

> **?** WORDS TO KNOW . . .
>
> emissions (i-MISH-uhnz)
>
> things that are sent off or out, such as gases

87

▲ Slag from this iron mine pollutes the soil.

nitrogen, and chlorine combine with oxygen in the air. The acids exist with water vapor in our **atmosphere.** When rain falls, so does the acid. Acid rain destroys trees, poisons rivers and lakes, and kills plants and animals.

Gold mining in the Amazon River has a nasty side effect: mercury poisoning. Miners use mercury, a liquid metal, to draw tiny gold particles from Amazon River silt. Mercury pours back into the water, polluting the river and its neighboring wetlands. Mercury poisons people as

> **?** **WORDS TO KNOW . . .**
>
> **atmosphere (AT-muhss-fihr)** the layer of gases that surrounds the earth

well as giant river otters, capybaras, and tapirs. Amazon River gold comes at a heavy cost to the environment.

Animals for Sale

A huge market exists for selling exotic animals. Parrots, macaws, rosellas, cockatoos, and other tropical birds are netted and sold as pets. Boas, anacondas, and other tropical snakes find themselves living in aquarium tanks instead of rain forests.

Boreal forests abound with fur-bearing animals. Minks, ermines, foxes, beavers, and martens are killed for their skins. The furs provide coats, muffs, and hats for fashionable dressers. In rain forests, tigers, leopards, and other cats are killed for their fur. Poachers slay crocodiles, snakes, and caimans for skins to make belts, shoes, and wallets.

In 1973, a meeting was held to stop the sale of endangered and

> **! WOULD YOU BELIEVE?**
>
> The greatest threat to many primate species is research laboratories. Scientists use lab monkeys to test medicines, makeup, shampoos, and other substances. Conservation groups believe this testing is cruel. They encourage using products labeled, "No animal testing is done to produce this product."

Minks like this cuddly pair belong ▸ in forests—not in cages.

threatened animals and animal parts. From that meeting, the Convention of International Trade in Endangered Species of Wild Fauna and Flora (CITES) was formed. By the early 1990s, 107 countries agreed to CITES rules. Now there are 160 members. The countries said they would stop selling ivory, fur, and parts from endangered animals, including many species of live monkeys, apes, and tropical birds.

CITES also supports captive breeding programs in zoos throughout the world. These breeding programs have increased populations of marmosets and Rhesus monkeys. CITES has built breeding ranches for crocodiles.

Poaching continues for one main reason: money. Poachers can earn more money selling a dozen exotic parrots than they could make in a lifetime of farming. This is true for every species poached. In addition, laws that try to stop the sale of animals and animal parts are only partly successful. Smuggling rare animals continues because there are willing buyers. As long as people buy crocodile shoes, leopard coats, or ivory carvings, poaching will not end.

Forests in Our Future

The world's forests face a bleak future. People need wood for fuel, building, furniture, and papermaking. Forests provide wood. Replanting efforts are important, but new-growth forests take a long time

▲ The Ozarks National Forest in Arkansas is one of many forest areas preserved by the U.S. government.

to produce wood. In many countries, logging companies do not replant forests.

There are 2,300 animals and 24,000 plants listed as endangered species. Newly discovered plants and animals are found all the time. Yet, forest destruction takes place so fast that many new species are gone before they are even named.

Saving forests depends on human interest. People need to protect our forests before there are no forests left to protect.

Chart of Species

CONTINENT	KEYSTONE SPECIES	FLAGSHIP SPECIES	UMBRELLA SPECIES	INDICATOR SPECIES
AFRICA	leaf-cutter and other ants, termites, bats, fig trees	lowland **gorillas**, mountain **gorillas**, leopards, chimpanzees	gorillas, chimpanzees	bees, butterflies, moths, bats
ASIA	Asian elephants, fig trees, bamboo, bats	Siberian tigers, Bengal tigers, Asian elephants, orangutans, giant pandas	Asiatic black bears, Javan rhinos, Sumatran rhinos, Siberian tigers, Bengal tigers	Javan gibbons, bees, moths, butterflies
AUSTRALIA	strangler fig trees, cassowaries, termites, bats	koala bears, quokkas, musky rat kangaroos, **lyrebirds**	cassowaries	boreal owls, bees, butterflies, moths
EUROPE	European **beavers**, beech **trees**, bees, bats	midwife **toads**, hazel hens, ladyslipper **orchids**	capercaillies, stag **beetles**, great spotted **woodpeckers**	bats, bees, beetles, moths, butterflies, pine martens, capercaillies
NORTH AMERICA	wolves, quaking aspens, brown bears, oak trees	wolves, mountain lions, bears, northern spotted owls	bears, northern spotted owls, gray wolves, red wolves	Boreal owls, wolverines, Mexican spotted owls
SOUTH AMERICA	leaf cutter ants, bats, fig trees, rain forest **trees**	**golden lion tamarins, jaguars,** Andes condors	**jaguars,** muriqui, Andes condors	bees, hummingbirds, butterflies, moths

▲ The above chart gives a starting point for identifying key species. Each forest environment has its own key species. The above chart lists some of those species.

[Bold-faced entries are the ones discussed in the text.]